A Day in the Life of a Bald Eagle

Julie Murray

Abdo Kids Junior
is an Imprint of Abdo Kids
abdobooks.com

Abdo
A DAY IN THE LIFE
OF AN ANIMAL
Kids

abdobooks.com

Published by Abdo Kids, a division of ABDO, P.O. Box 398166, Minneapolis, Minnesota 55439.

Printed in the United States of America, North Mankato, Minnesota.

102025

012026

Photo Credits: Getty Images, Shutterstock

Production Contributors: Teddy Borth, Jennie Forsberg, Grace Hansen

Design Contributors: Candice Keimig, Pakou Moua

Library of Congress Control Number: 2025936505

Publisher's Cataloging-in-Publication Data

Names: Murray, Julie, author.

Title: A day in the life of a bald eagle / by Julie Murray

Description: Minneapolis, Minnesota : Abdo Kids, 2026 | Series: A day in the life of an animal | Includes online resources and index.

Identifiers: ISBN 9798384907282 (lib. bdg.) | ISBN 9798384907985 (ebook) | ISBN 9798384908333 (read-to-me ebook)

Subjects: LCSH: Bald eagle--Juvenile literature. | Birds of prey--Juvenile literature. | Birds--Juvenile literature. | Birds--Behavior--Juvenile literature. | Animal behavior--Juvenile literature. | Ornithology--Juvenile literature.

Classification: DDC 598.943--dc23

Table of Contents

A Bald Eagle's Day

The sun is rising. The bald eagle starts its day.

5

It stands in its nest. The nest is high in a tree.

The bald eagle looks around. The **eaglets** are safe! It is time to hunt.

The bald eagle flies over the water and trees. It hunts for food.

It **swoops** into the river.

It grabs a fish.

It flies back to the nest.

The **eaglets** eat.

It is time to rest. The young eagles sleep close together.

The bald eagle hunts again. It grabs a **rodent** to eat.

The day is ending. The eagle settles in its nest.

Bald Eagle Facts

Bright yellow beak and feet

Lives for up to 30 years in the wild

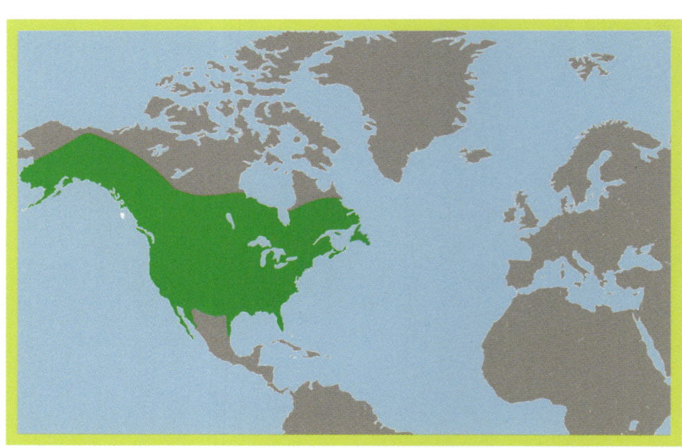

Lives throughout North America

Up to 8-foot (2.5 m) long wingspan

Glossary

eaglet
a young eagle.

rodent
a small mammal, such as a mouse or rat.

swoop
to sweep down suddenly from above.

Index

Visit **abdokids.com** to access crafts, games, videos, and more!

Use Abdo Kids code

AAK7282

or scan this QR code!